Miller's work stands out like a Thoroughbred in a pen full of ponies. His wry humor works the same way that Baxter Black's does—it saves us from taking ourselves too seriously.

— Gary Vorhes, former Editor-in-Chief
Western Horseman magazine

A true westerner to the core and one who's "made a hand" as a scribe as well, Rod Miller is that rare breed who blends artistic sensibility with cowboy attitude. He's funny and serious and hits all the marks in-between, and always in that high-quality, polished verse he writes—the kind that looks as effortless as a great bronc ride, but is every bit as tough to pull off as that ride was.

— Jesse Mullins, Jr., founding editor,
American Cowboy magazine

Reading Rod Miller's poems is like getting a giant box of candy.... I always look forward to his contributions. I particularly enjoy the ironic humor and admire his sophisticated use of the language, which he somehow manages to present in a completely accessible way. We get many poems that have the feeling of being "dashed off." And then we get poems like Rod's! It's a pleasure.

—Margo Metegrano
CowboyPoetry.com

Things a COWBOY SEES
and other poems

By Rod Miller

*Dedicated to
Jesse Mullins, Jr.,
the editor who first saw fit to
apply ink to my poetry.*

THINGS A COWBOY SEES AND OTHER POEMS
By Rod Miller
Published by Port Yonder Press
Shellsburg, Iowa
www.PortYonderPress.com
ISBN 9781935600077
Copyright © 2011 by Rod Miller

All rights reserved. No part of this book may be reproduced or transmitted in any form or by any means, electronic or mechanical, including photocopying and recording, or by any information storage or retrieval system, without permission in writing from the publisher.

Edited by Chila Woychik

Cover design by behindthegift.com

Cover photo ©James Fain

Printed in USA

Port Yonder Press has given this book a rating of PG13 for language and thematic elements.

Acknowledgments

As with any literary work, many people contributed to this collection of poetry, some in ways they are not aware of. I would like to acknowledge a few of those.

The book is dedicated to Jesse Mullins, longtime editor of *American Cowboy* magazine. I owe my first published poem, and many others that made it into print, to Jesse. Gary Vorhes, and, later, A. J. Mangum, editors at *Western Horseman* magazine, also published several of my poems, as did C. J. Hadley of *Range* magazine. I owe them all a debt of gratitude for lending credibility to the idea that I could be a poet.

Special thanks is due Margo Metegrano, the brains and brawn behind the world's largest cowboy poetry web site, CowboyPoetry.com. Margo's contributions to the art of cowboy poetry are beyond comprehension, as is the attention she has paid me. From encouraging my submissions to bestowing honors to promoting my writing successes in other media to featuring the essays I've penned on writing poetry to arranging introductions to other poets, her support has been more than deserved or expected, and much appreciated.

Many, many poets, living and dead, have lent assistance, if only by inspiring me to write harder in an attempt to reach their level. Some have become friends. While I cannot name them all, they include, in alphabetical order, S. Omar Barker, Baxter Black, Laurie Wagner Buyer, Charles Badger Clark, Doris Daley, Janice Gilbertson, DW Groethe, Yvonne Hollenbeck, Don Kennington, Phil Kennington, JoLynne Kirkwood, Bruce Kiskaddon, Mike Logan, Wallace McRae, Jane Morton, A. B. "Banjo" Paterson, Vess Quinlan, Buck Ramsey, Pat Richardson, Red Shuttleworth, Red Steagall, and Andy Wilkinson.

Paul Zarzyski and Bob Schild merit special mention, both because of the personal time, attention, and kindness they showed a bothersome novice poet and because much of their poetry is inspired by their time in the rodeo arena, memories of which also triggers many of my poems.

Thanks to Chila Woychik and her saddle pals at Port Yonder Press for their willingness to publish a book of cowboy poetry (few publishers are brave enough to take on such a job) and their hard work to make it a better book than it deserves to be.

Finally, thanks to my wife, Susan, and daughters Kate and Lisa, who try not to bother me when I try to write. And to my dad and mom, Howard and Renee, who brought me into a cowboy world and allowed me to grow up in it—a fact I did not appreciate enough at the time.

Some of the poems in this collection appeared in other publications, occasionally in slightly altered form:

"Cowboy, Defined," "The Cowboy Trail," "The E.S.L. Ranch," "Irons in the Fire," "Landing Gear," "Looper Blues," "Why I'm Not a Roper," and "Ranked Among the Top 15 Automobiles of All Time" appeared in *American Cowboy* magazine.

"The E.S.L. Ranch" appeared in the anthology *The Big Roundup*.

"Outlaw" appeared in *Cowboy Magazine*.

"Rodeo Regina" appeared in the anthology *Cowboys are Part Human*.

"Cowboy Coffee" appeared in *Cowboys are Part Human*,

Cowboys and Cookouts, and *Elko Daily Free Press*.

"Rhyme of the Ancient Trail Driver" appeared in the *Denver Post* and *Elko Daily Free Press*.

"Bad Road" and "Things a Cowboy Sees" appeared in *New Plains Review*.

"A Bolt of Broomtails" and "Go Home Again" appeared in the anthology *New Poets of the American West*.

"Gone to Town," "Morning Glory," "Road Warriors," "The Staff of Life," and "Work Ethic" appeared in *Range* magazine.

"Beauty is Only Skin Deep," "Long May It Wave," and "Why I'm Not a Roper," appeared in *Rope Burns*.

"Feral" and "Number 16" appeared in *Roundup Magazine*.

"A Guide to ranching for the Politically Correct," "Hot Time," "Luck (But Not Exactly the Beginner's Kind)," "No Enjoyment in Unemployment," "Number 16," and "My Memories are Looking Up," appeared in *Western Horseman* magazine.

Table of Contents

I. Horses and Hosses

A Bolt of Broomtails	24
Feral	25
Haiku for a Horseback Morning	26
Beauty is Only Skin Deep *(But Ugly Goes All the Way Through)*	27
Last Full Measure of Devotion	28
Eternal Flame	29
My Memories are Looking Up	30
Grounded	32

II. Life Out West

Morning Glory	34
A Guide to Ranching for the Politically Correct	35
A Little Madness in the Spring	38
Irons in the Fire	39
Hot Time	40
Indelible	42
Road Warriors	43
Meadow Hay	44
Baptism	45
Work Ethic	46
Things a Cowboy Sees	48
The E.S.L. Ranch	50
Forecast	52
No Enjoyment in Unemployment	53
Gates Left Open	55
Buckaroo	56
Haiku for a Former Rounder	58
Gone to Town	59
Go Home Again	60

III. The Rodeo Road

Bad Road 62
Rodeo Regina 64
Landing Gear 65
Why I'm Not a Roper 66
Rodeo Rhythm 67
Looper Blues 69
Womb to Tomb...70
Long May It Wave 71
Luck (But Not Exactly the Beginner's Kind) 72
Ranked Among the Top 15 Automobiles of All Time............74
Number 16 75

IV. Roundups and Trail Drives

Rhyme of the Ancient Trail Driver 78
Brother's Keeper 79
Cowboy Coffee 80
Outlaw 81
Tabula Rasa..84
Trail Driving Days 86
The Cowboy Trail 88

V. MAKING A HAND

Cowboy, Defined	92
Packsaddle	93
Resolution	94
The Staff of Life	95
About the Author	96

An Introduction
to Cowboy Poetry in General and This Collection in Particular

Long, long ago in a time before iPods, before cell phones, before Blackberries, when there was no satellite television, no on-demand movies, no YouTube, people had to devise their own entertainments. Before America was wired, back when we were unplugged, people took every opportunity to get together, enjoy each other's company, and amuse one another.

At any moment, in any crowd—in a parlor, a schoolhouse, a grange hall, around a campfire—someone was likely to offer a soliloquy from Shakespeare, someone else might sing a favorite song. And you'd likely hear a recitation of a poem. Schoolchildren routinely memorized long passages of plays and prose and poetry and offered them in public interpretation; grownups continued the tradition.

While echoes of those bygone days of homemade entertainment remain, it's a tradition that's largely forgotten in our tuned-in society. And one place you'll hear those echoes is in the tradition of cowboy poetry. There are hundreds, probably thousands, of men and women who, at the drop of a wide-brimmed hat, will happily reel off a rhyme for anyone who'll listen. They'll recite "classic" poems from the cowboy catalog, more modern compositions they've gathered from other poets, and creations of their own. They'll flock together at hundreds of appointed times and places all across the country to share verses with one another and audiences that range from a handful to standing-room-only auditoriums.

It can be argued that cowboy poetry presented in public recitations paved the way for a renaissance, of sorts, for spoken poetry. Other than a few scholarly conclaves, where academic poets read mostly droning, angst-ridden free-verse selections to one another and few others, there was a dearth of poetry for public consumption in the decades between the disappearance of the finger-snapping beat poets of the 1950s and cowboy poetry's appearance on the scene in the 1980s. Its continuing, even growing, popularity very likely played a role in the advent of today's slam poetry phenomenon.

So where did cowboy poetry come from, and why?

Early Days

Let's go back, briefly, to those days when memorization and recitation of poetry and other literary works was popular. Cowboy work involves long hours on horseback or in isolated camps, leaving those who herd cattle alone with their thoughts for extended periods—a perfect situation for learning popular poems and other recitations, and even creating original works. Then, evenings around campfires and in bunkhouses provided ample opportunities to share verses committed to memory. Popular poems—and songs and tall tales—got passed around from ranch to ranch, town to town, and became entrenched in the tradition.

Some of those poems from the earliest years found their way into the permanence of print; most simply disappeared along with those who recited them.

The "Golden Age" of cowboy poetry came a few decades after the demise of the trail-drive era that defines our cowboy mythology. Nostalgia for the "disappearing West" led to widespread writing of reminiscences, memoirs, songs, and poems by and for people longing for those bygone days. Poems about cowboy life and the Old West were published in magazines and newspapers, on calendars and post cards, in collections and anthologies, and on practically anything else ink would stick to. The best of the poems from that era survive, and still please audiences at cowboy poetry gatherings and performances today.

Some were penned by real cowboys—men like Bruce Kiskaddon

and Carmen William "Curley" Fletcher who knew the cowboy life firsthand. Charles Badger Clark and S. Omar Barker had limited connections with cowboy work, but their poems were and are extremely popular. Some, such as E. A. Brininstool and Henry Herbert Knibbs, were mere observers of the American cowboy, but managed to pen poetry authentic enough to be appreciated by cowboys. And some ever-popular poets among the cowboy crowd, most notably A. B. "Banjo" Paterson and Will Ogilvie, never saw a cowboy in his natural state on a ranch on the Western range, but created outstanding rhymes based on the similar experiences of "drovers" on "cattle stations" in the Australian "bush" or "outback."

Almost any gathering of cowboy poets will include recitations of the works of some of those "classic" poets (or others) along with poems of more recent vintage and original compositions by the reciters.

Revival

But how, and why, did cowboy poetry survive the demise of public recitation and other homespun entertainments once so commonplace? It all comes down to a cold winter day in Elko, Nevada, in 1985. And, of course, a lot of preparatory work to get to that day.

A couple of academic folklorists, Hal Cannon and Jim Griffith, were intrigued with cowboy poetry as a folk art, and their studies revealed there were still a few cowboys who maintained the art, memorizing old poems and reciting them in barrooms and bunkhouses. Some, they learned, also wrote poems of their own, often in secret, occasionally with some embarrassment, usually unaware that other cowboys did the same.

With the help of folklorists across the West, Cannon and Griffith scoured the wide-open spaces to locate cowboys afflicted with poesy and invited them to gather in Elko that winter day to share and compare. And so they did, with a handful of poets swapping lines for friends, families, one another, and a few hundred curious onlookers.

For reasons no one understands—including the people who invented the event—the cowboy poetry gathering caught on, and the second annual became the third annual and, in 2011, the twenty-seventh annual and counting. More remarkable is the fact that similar gatherings emerged across the West, spread to the Midwest and even the East, and into Canada. And while events come and go, many are but a few years behind Elko in longevity.

Along with the growth of cowboy poetry gatherings came the emergence of cowboy poets. There seems to be no shortage of folks with a hankering to stand on a stage and share a poem. From working cowboys to part-time cowboys to those raised in a cowboy environment who've moved on to other lives in the cities to people who don't even know which end of a cow gets up first, the desire to recite strikes all kinds.

"Poets" and Poets

A few—not nearly enough—of these newly minted poets learn and share the best poems from the classic era. (Oddly enough, the term cowboy "poet" applies equally to those who write poems, and to reciters who have never written a word.) But most write their own stuff. And here, I believe, is where today's cowboy poetry departs from that of the past.

While cowboy poetry—all poetry, for that matter—was born in the spoken word, it became, and achieved permanence as, a literary art. No one will ever hear—or read—many of those "oral tradition" poems composed and recited and passed around in the late 1800s because they were never put on paper. But the work of the "classic" cowboy poets is still with us because they were *writers*. They wrote to be published, and the permanence of their poems (beyond their inherent literary quality) came through widespread distribution in print. If any of those early-day poets stumped the countryside spouting poems from the stage, there is no record of it. (Possible exceptions are Badger Clark and S. Omar Barker, both of whom were popular public speakers and included poems in their presentations.)

Many of today's cowboy poets, on the other hand, care little for the written word. They're out to become stage-show entertainers, so effective recitation takes priority. Rather than poetry, much of what they write might more properly be called "material."

It's partly market-driven—the popularity of cowboy poetry gatherings created the situation. More cowboy poetry fans are willing to shell out for tickets to a gathering or for a recording than for a book. There are hundreds of opportunities for "poets" to get on stage in front an audience; opportunities to see your poetry in print are few and far between. Most poetry books, mostly self-published, sell few copies, so today's poets are more likely to record their recitations and sell them on CD.

It can be argued, then, that cowboy poetry today is more a performance art than a literary art. If you tell someone you're a cowboy poet, the automatic assumption is that you have a memorized repertoire of poems you can recite on demand. Where those poems come from—whether they are classics or your own compositions—is of little interest.

For the most part, a poem's entertainment value is now more important than its literary value. This inevitably has changed today's cowboy poetry when compared to those well-written, carefully crafted "classics." Many of today's poems, even if popular in recitation, do not always stand up on the page.

A Gathering of Poems

While I often conduct workshops and give lectures, and sometimes read poems in public, the performance trail is not one I have followed—at least as a performer. I admire a good recitation more than most and have enjoyed more cowboy poetry performances than I can remember, but I prefer to sit in the audience rather than stand on the stage. Part of the reason is disposition, but it's mostly a matter of time and energy. Good reciters spend countless hours and lots of brain power memorizing and rehearsing poems.

I would rather spend that time writing. And reading. And learning.

Fortunately, cowboy poetry today is not *all* performance. There are still cowboy poets for whom writing matters: poets who craft verse that reads as well as it recites. Those are the poets, along with those from cowboy poetry's Golden Age, I learn from and look to for inspiration and direction.

In my poems, I attempt at various times to tackle time-honored subjects and emulate traditional and rhyme-and-meter styles, as well as follow the lead of the modern cowboy and Western poets who experiment with subject matter and form. The results are, as most poets will confess, lacking. For while writing poetry can be satisfying, the poems themselves are often unsatisfactory. Such is the bane of anyone who attempts to create something worthwhile out of a blank page and the twenty-six letters of the alphabet.

This collection features some of my best attempts. From the lighthearted to the contemplative, traditional to experimental, formal to unstructured, it is a representative travelogue of my journey through cowboy and Western poetry. So far.

Thanks for coming along for the ride.

—Rod Miller, Sandy, Utah, 2011

Note: Much of this Introduction appeared as a Foreword to a special section on cowboy and Western poetry in the Spring, 2010, issue of New Plains Review.

Horses and Hosses

Rod Miller

A Bolt of Broomtails

Across alkali flat and sandhill,
over the sage-covered plain
the mesteñada flows like fabric,
dancing ahead of its dusty train.

> *chestnut, claybank,*
> *coyote dun,*
> *buckskin, black,*
> *blue roan, bay,*
> *piebald, palomino,*
> *pinto, paint,*
> *grulla, ghost white,*
> *dapple gray*

Rippling in the morning light
the hues shimmer and shift;
mustangs run as colored threads
through the warp and weft.

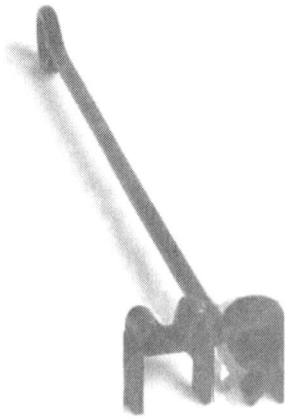

FERAL

Heart made of rawhide
hardened in the fires of hell,
he sights down the barrel cold-eyed
and chambers another shell.

Desert breath dries mud
puddled downhill from wounds
weeping mustang blood
that darkens the dunes.

Lead lashes out, a mare bawls.
Her foal trembles, dying inside
as, gutshot, she staggers and falls,
piling dust in muzzle slide.

Life leaks out. Death creeps in.
A soul grown cold and stiff.
When you earn the wages of sin
payment is a matter of when, not if.

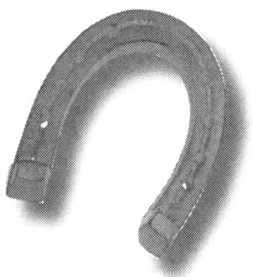

Haiku for a Horseback Morning
Rod Miller

Fetlocks sponge up dew,
waking trail through silver'd green
until the sun climbs.

Things a COWBOY SEES *and other poems*

Beauty is Only Skin Deep
(But Ugly Goes All the Way Through)

Ewe-neck, cow hocked, mule-hips, hog-back—
hell, you can hardly tell she's a horse.
My saddle pals call her a waste of tack.
She's so ugly stud horses file for divorce.

Her pasterns slope at such an odd angle
I fear collapse could come any time.
She's gotch-eared so bad that they dangle
above pig eyes 'bout the size of a dime.

Cold jawed, stump-sucking, buzzard bait.
Long in the tooth with a hard, smooth mouth.
A fiddle-footed winger with a paddling gait
that simultaneously travels east and south.

A hammer-headed, hay-burning bangtail
afraid of cattle, snorty, and rope shy.
The only reason this plug ain't for sale
is there's a limit to how much I'll lie.

So dozy you might mistake her for dead;
a damn poor specimen of the equine race.
But the sad fact is, this wall-eyed jughead
is the best horse I've got on the place.

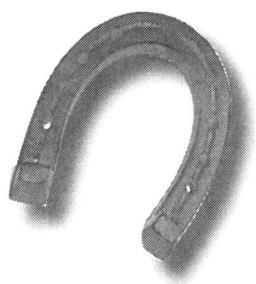

Rod Miller
Last Full Measure of Devotion

It makes no sense that an assemblage of bones
stacked unsteady, fragile, on final fingernails
    too small for the bulk and susceptible to stones
will run, trot, walk, plod, stumble along trails
    steep, deep, rough, narrow, of dust, rock, mud;
sweat ground down to lather, shredded breath
    sucked through dilated nostrils rimming blood,
struggling under saddle, ridden, willingly, to death.

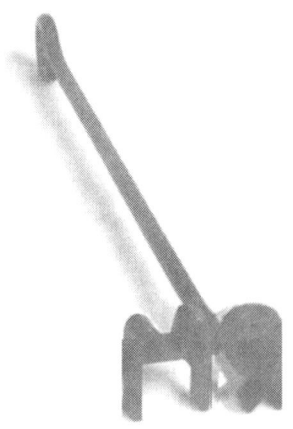

Things a COWBOY SEES and other poems
Eternal Flame

A chaos of bones in the brush
on the sandhill in the far
corner of the pasture.
Ride out. See the rodeo star.

She was found stiff and cold
under a shroud of snow
by the hands on the feed
wagon three winters ago,

closing out a long retirement
in that field. For fifteen years
she'd gone down the road.
Seemed to crave those cheers

when she'd unload a bronc
rider before whistle sound.
Many a cowboy hit paydirt,
but more hit the ground.

Then it was gone. She lost it
all. Except the fire in her eyes.
It's still there. Even in death
it's hot enough to cauterize.

Ride out. Find her skull.
Where once burned live coals,
now, fiery against bleached bone,
Indian Paintbrush fills eye holes.

My Memories are Looking Up

Rod Miller

Every horse is different.
No two are the same.
Ask most any cowboy—
there'll be dozens he can name.

You recall them by their color;
by blazes, stars, and snips.
By the way they carry their ears.
The angle of their hips.

You remember how they travel.
Recollect how they take the bits.
Call to mind the slope of withers
and how the saddle sits.

Those that try to snatch a bite
while walking through tall grass.
Some wind-sucking cribbers.
Others, windy with gas.

You know some who take to water
and some who shy away.
Some who are scared of cattle.
Some who'll buck you off for play.

My memory is especially full
of horses that pitch and fight,
separating me from the saddle
and allowing in daylight.

So I've often been flat on my back
and know the view from there;
I recall more horses than I care to
by the look of their belly hair:

The distinctive hues and shades.
The curlicues and swirls.
The blotches and the splotches.
The cowlicks, waves, and whorls.

Yes, I remember lots of nasty broncs.
But I wish that I'd forgot 'em—
'cause it really ain't The Cowboy Way
to recollect them from the bottom.

Rod Miller
Grounded

There's just one thing to do
with a colt fourteen-two
that bucks twice as high as the sky:
turn the nails upside down,
tack his shoes to the ground,
so he's spiked to the earth and can't fly.

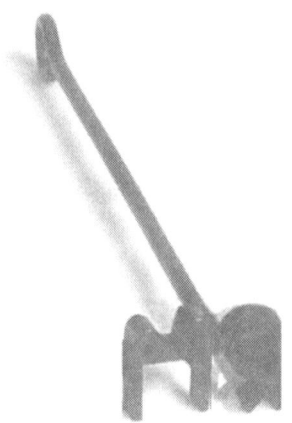

Life Out West

Morning Glory

Rod Miller

Stars punch holes in the dark and
the moon curls on the sky like
a hoof paring from a soft-footed horse
while razor-edged peaks stand
against the ribbon of dawn, a dike
holding the morning from its course.

Atop Long Ridge we squat
and sit and roll and spit. Lies hang
in the air, drifting like powder smoke
from round after round of bull shot.
Sparks glint when steel shoes clang
impatient against stone. Scrub oak

materializes deliberately out of the dim
and quakies on the ridges appear.
Stirrup fenders slap saddle seats,
latigos slide cinches taut. A final brim
tug and chap buckle snug and my rear
meets leather. A hesitant sun greets

the crew. Light crawls slow where
today's gather will take us, away
from Long Ridge and our dark climb.
I glory in our forty minutes there;
glad we arrived too early in the day
(or late at night) to get to work on time.

Things a COWBOY SEES and other poems

A Guide to Ranching for the Politically Correct

When we first got into ranching
we really didn't expect
to see the business change so much
to become politically correct.

Cowboy lingo was simple then.
It was easy to communicate.
But now you can't say what you mean,
you're forced to obfuscate

so you don't do irreparable damage
to some critter's self esteem,
and to protect their tender feelings
you must be gentle in the extreme.

"Cowboy" is the first of many words
that we've been forced to shun.
It's sexist as well as sexually confused
and has been replaced by Cattleperson.

We no longer call them "Dogies,"
those calves without a mother.
We merely say they're Victims of
a Parental Deficit Disorder.

And "Cull" is an insensitive way
to describe a worn-out cow;
Candidates for Outplacement
is what we call them now.

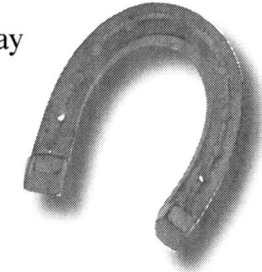

If you say you're raising "Fat Steers"
their feelings you might addle,
so we don't talk about their weight—
they're Fitness Challenged Cattle.

And Sexually Neutral Bovine is
the term we've adopted here
to avoid damaging the confidence
of what once was called a "Steer."

"Heifer" is another of those sexist terms
that crosses the P.C. line,
so we've dropped that one in favor of
Pre-Pubescent Female Bovine.

Then there's that label "Herd Bull"
that doesn't pass the test.
That job is now described as
Serially Monogamous Fertilization Specialist.

Being accused of racism is
another thing we dread,
so Multicultural Cattle is how we refer
to those who were once "Crossbred."

They may question their femininity
if you label cows as "Drys."
Calling them Inactive Lactators
is a change we feel is wise.

Sending an animal to the "Sick Pen"
is sure to affect its composure;
a gentler way of describing it is as
the Healing Enclosure.

We say the cattle on our ranch are
Preparing for a Career in Food Service
because we fear a word like "Beef"
will frighten, and make them nervous.

Gentle. Sensitive. Caring. Concerned.
Those words define our place.
And the terms we use to describe our work
are chosen for charm and grace.

But I'd as soon go back to Ranching
the way it used to be,
instead of Hosting this Politically Correct
Ruminant Residential Facility.

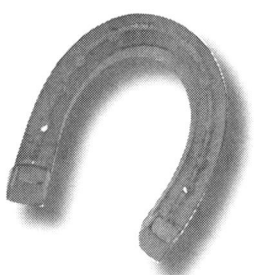

Rod Miller
A Little Madness in the Spring

The sun, rested and ready after
a lazy winter down south,
clawing higher up the side of the sky,
working longer days. Eager mouths

sucking growth into the upper
pasture. Sated with life: playing,
bucking, chasing over grass
pouring out of the ground. Saying

nothing, we admire clean, soft
hides shimmering in fresh light.
They hold no memories of gore,
of a slimy passage in the night;

ours, alone, the remembering of
lantern glow, watching cows bring
forth yearly wages. Only knowing
smiles pass our lips after 23 Springs.

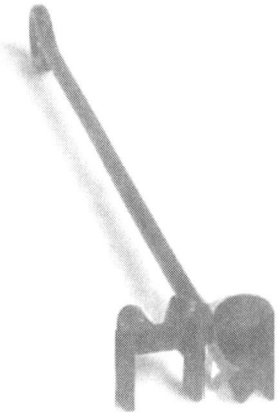

Irons in the Fire

Branding at the home place was always a family
   affair,
only three dozen calves a year ever needed burnt
   hair.
The girls would rope a hind leg and snub it to the
   post,
the boys would tail the calves down and hold them
   there to roast
Under the red-hot stamp brand from the fire that
   Mother stoked;
Dad handled the iron; the calves, they bawled and
   smoked.
We'd inject them all with vaccine and crop off their
   left ears
and turn all the feisty bull calves into docile steers.
It was a job that had to be done, but it always
   seemed like play—
we did more bonding than branding, there at the old
   home place.

Rod Miller

Hot Time

I bucked off my horse this morning
and painfully damaged my pride.
Then I poked a thumb in my dallies
and peeled off most of the hide.

I'm walking crooked 'cause my back
went out in the middle of tailing one down,
and I've been run over so many times
that I rattle like a rodeo clown.

I got too close to a nervous old cow
while pushing a bunch through the gate
and got hosed down with a long green stream
that covered me boot heels to pate.

There's a rock-hard lump in my forearm
where the vaccine gun went astray,
and about half a brand on my instep
that probably won't go away.

I cut my finger while castrating and
went lightheaded from loss of blood.
I inhaled so much corral dust that
my lungs are still heavy with mud.

I got kicked in the jaw by a heifer
and was too sore at dinner to eat
so I just stretched out in the shade for
a nap, then had to be helped to my feet.

But I got a second wind for the afternoon
and waded back into the fray,
to be kicked and stomped and rope burned
some more to finish out the day.

Then I collapsed in pain against the fence,
so weak I needed help to open a beer.
Still, I wouldn't miss branding for anything
— it's the most fun I have all year.

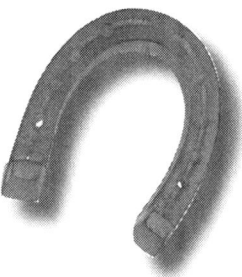

Rod Miller

Indelible

Memories linger long
of the
    dust in the air
    sweat in your hat
    mud in your eyes
    blisters in your boots
    blood on your blue jeans
    shit on your shirt
    beller in your ears
    grit on your gums
    steel in your teeth
    hocks in your hand…
but the burnt-hair
    smoke in your nose
is as permanent as a brand.

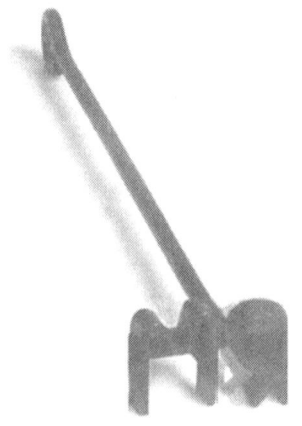

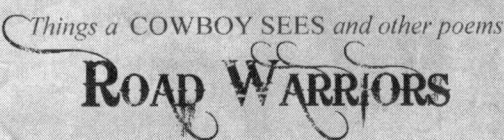

Road Warriors

On narrow country roads
opposing pickup trucks
stop side by side.

Drivers roll down windows
 aim elbows at each other .
  and shoot the bull.

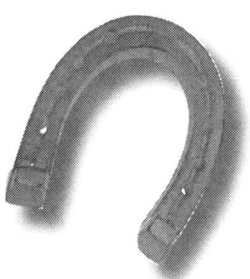

Rod Miller

Meadow Hay

Stem by stem, blade by blade,
bowing to the cutter bar as
the tractor, an insignificant dot,
crawls around the sixty-acre plot.

Defenseless against spinning tines,
the grass winds and coils into
an endless rope dragged by the rake,
hay in the tractor's wake.

Yellow teeth chomp hungrily
and droppings litter the ground
as the baler, appetite unsatisfied,
nips at the tractor's backside.

Bawling cows in tow, the tractor
returns the summer meadow—
stacked against winter cold—to its own,
four stomachs from home.

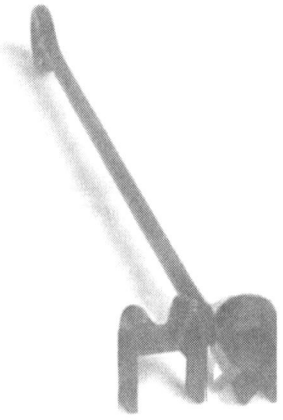

Things a COWBOY SEES *and other poems*

Baptism

Come Saturday night
I heat some water
and fill the old bathtub,
stretch out in the steam
to soak my bones and
give my body a scrub

and scrape off the stink
of a long week's work
before heading into town
in fresh-laundered clothes
and polished boots and a
pickup just hosed down.

Then I join the gather
at the Roundup Bar
to talk and drink and eat,
all clean and pure and
shaved and scrubbed
and smelling oh-so sweet.

It's important, you see,
to be washed clean
for the company I keep—
there'd be no forgiveness
from my cowboy friends
if they knew I herded sheep.

Work Ethic

Rod Miller

He was a ranch hand from the old school
who didn't take to modern ways.
He never seemed to be pressured by
fleeting minutes, hours, or days.
Why, I'd find him napping under a tree
shaded up from the afternoon sun;
awakened, he'd invite me to join him,
and insist that the work would get done.

He spoiled my kids and my horses.
Shared morning coffee with my wife.
Swore that rassling with kittens and pups
was as good as it gets in this life.
I'd catch him a-sitting on a ridge line
just watching the rise of the sun;
he'd tell me, sit a spell and enjoy the show,
and insist that the work would get done.

He'd only work cattle on horseback;
plumb refused to mount a four-wheeler—
swore them noisy infernal machines were
too rank for an old bronc peeler.
I'd find him of an evening on the top rail,
face aglow in the low-hanging sun;
he'd brush off my reminder about the chores
and insist that the work would get done.

Many a day he'd stop the feed wagon
to watch the calves buck and play,
and he'd shut down the baler while haying
just to shoo a scared rabbit away.
He was a constant source of frustration
'til we buried him 'neath a cold winter sun.
And I hear Granddad yet from beyond the
grave, insisting that the work will get done.

Rod Miller

Things a Cowboy Sees

Hung up on the jagged peaks
the sun begins the day,
breaks loose and climbs the morning sky,
burning night's cold away.

The horse 'tween your knees snorts the
cool air, hops and kicks at the blue.
But you don't mind. He's just glad to be alive
and today, you feel that way too.

Cows abandon the watering hole;
in single file they march away,
up the worn trail toward the hills
as giddy calves buck and play.

Then like a frayed old catch rope
the trail begins to unravel.
The cows separate as the track unbraids,
each choosing a strand to travel.

Ahead, a meadowlark flops around, wing
wobbling like a broken dry stick.
She takes to the air as you ride near;
lands, and repeats her trick.

The patch burnt by last summer's lightning,
just beyond the saddleback pass,
is rising like phoenix from the ashes,
haired over by tender green grass.

That three-legged coyote's in the meadow,
a field mouse trapped 'tween her paws.
Its tail in her teeth, she tosses it high and
catches it with a snap of her jaws.

She ambles away in her own good time
like she don't even know you're there;
then glances back with a look that says
she knows, but doesn't care.

You put aside those overdue bills and the
banker you can't seem to please;
blinded, for a while, to life's burdens
by the things a cowboy sees.

The E.S.L.* Ranch

Stranded, I was, in some cow town,
out of work and down on my luck;
no way to pay for my next meal
with my finances at less than a buck

when a man drove up in a pickup truck,
said he was looking for a worker to hire.
Hauled me off to the middle of nowhere;
dumped me out next to a campfire.

I'd just settled in for a good night's sleep
to rest up for the coming day's work
when hell broke loose with a vengeance
and awakened me with a jerk.

Roll out, you waddy! some guy hollered,
can't ya hear coosie a-callin'?
Haul yerself out of them sougans!
Roll up that hen-skin and paulin!

Put on a load of Mexican strawberries
an' some sinkers to line yer flue,
then grab a kack and come on back
and I'll tell ya what you're to do.

*Rattle yer hocks down to the cavvy
an' with a reata snag a cayuse,
then light out into the brasada
and chouse any critters that's loose.*

I stammered at the man, dumbfounded.
He said, *There ain't no time fer palaver!
If ya wanna be a ranahan
get forked and get out on the gather!*

Well, I resigned my position on the spot,
mind reeling and spirit broken—
starving's easier than working a job
where English isn't spoken.

* English as a Second Language

Rod Miller
Forecast

Wrung out grass sags
under the weight of a sun
that burns every blade.
Leaves hang limp and
wilted on the trees,
curling, seeking shade.

The skin of the earth
a sea of begging bowls,
cracked and curved toward
rain that doesn't fall;
vainly petitioning a
sky dry, and hard.

Trails buried in powder
thick and fine, the verge
between solid ground
and dust indistinct,
softening rattling hoofs,
dampening sound.

He lifts his lid to mop
a pale brow, a gesture made
futile by lack of sweat;
tears, too, gone dry
in fear that this is not
as bad as it's going to get.

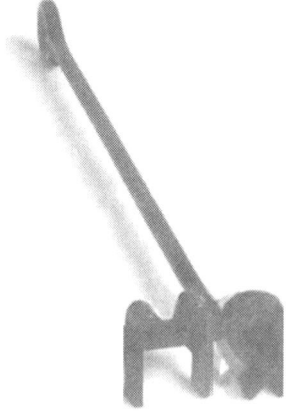

Things a COWBOY SEES *and other poems*

NO ENJOYMENT IN UNEMPLOYMENT

His staples won't stick to fence posts,
nor his brands to a slick calf's hide.
And I'm weary of hearing his lying boasts
about the rank broncs he can ride.

He never remembers to pack a lunch
and he's forever bummin' a smoke;
his turn to buy a round for the bunch
somehow always finds him broke.

His loops won't fit over a critter's head,
nor can they find their way to a hock.
He often gets lost right here on the spread
when sent out to gather stock.

The calves he castrates get infection.
The hay he bales turns to mold.
Colts he schools all need correction
if we hope to get them sold.

His saddle horses are cinch-galled
with sore backs and withers fistulous.
His lasso rope is so twisted and balled
and kinked and knotted it's ridiculous.

His tack is always in disrepair.
Horseshoes he nails on never fit.
Compare his saddle to his easy chair
and you'll see where he'd rather sit.

The chaps he borrowed have gone astray.
The spurs I loaned him are missing too.
And I have to follow him around every day
to do the jobs he forgets to do.

I guess you can see why I let him go;
he's the sorriest hand I've ever had.
But, still, I just can't help feeling low
about giving the sack to my Dad.

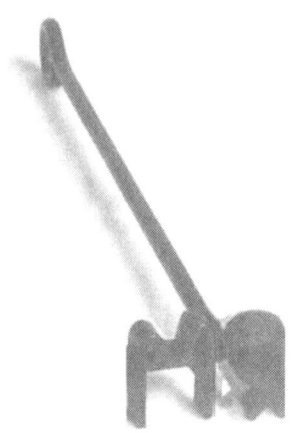

Gates Left Open

Between the furrows of
two-track roads
grass, once cropped by the
undercarriage of teams and wagons,
pickup trucks and trailers,
stands tall.

Feral cats echo through
dim barns and outbuildings,
sleek from the fat of the rats that
outbreed them.

Silted stock ponds trickle
dust into the wind, filtered through
rattling rushes and reeds
once lush.

Impenetrable tangles of thatch
choke thirsty roots rains
no longer reach.

Gates left open hold nothing for
there is nothing left to embrace—
emptiness runs free from one
pockmarked dun pasture
to the next.

Prairie dogs stand sentinel
over protected holes and hollows,
seeing nothing.

Rod Miller
Buckaroo

In chinks and wild rag,
silver spurs, battered hat,
leather cuffs, and vest
he smells of latigo,
horse sweat, and sage,
this postcard of the West.

In hot sun, cold wind,
rain and snow; in
dirt and dust and mud
from first light to last
it's hide and horns, and
shit and snot and blood.

On another man's land
and another man's horses,
punching another man's cattle
he's unfettered and free
with no ties that bind;
owns little else but a saddle.

If he tires of the scenery,
the foreman, the food, or
some greenhorn and his braggin'
he draws his pay, rides away,
and throws his bedroll
in another outfit's wagon.

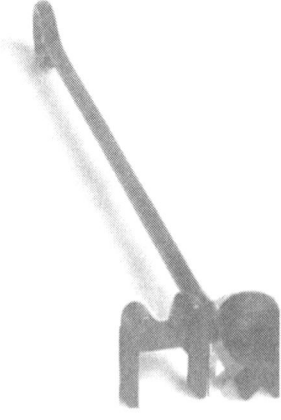

He ain't in it for money
for he'll never get rich.
And it's work not many will do.
But it's more than a job
to them that do it; it's a
calling, and it's called Buckaroo.

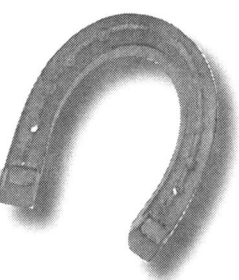

Haiku for a Former Rounder
Rod Miller

I was born to buck
but I've been broke to ride.
Done sold my saddle.

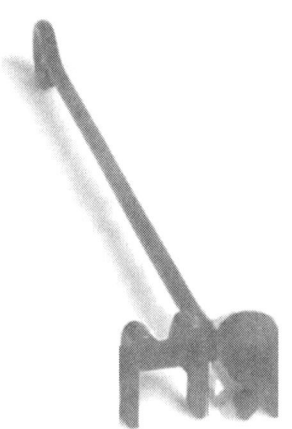

Gone to Town

The night sky isn't black,
it's a milky gray.
And it seems half the stars
have faded away.
Soles don't walk on the land.
Hands touch nothing real.
Asphalt. Iron. Concrete.
Plastic. Cold hard steel.
Horses live in boxes
locked away and bound,
turning nervous circles.
Cattle won't be found.
No smell of mother earth
when a wind blows by;
just stink and smoke and fumes
that water the eye.
Half my life, this city.
Home's not far from here—
two hours on the highway.
Takes you twenty years.

Rod Miller
Go Home Again

Pull the snap from the hasp and squeak
neglected hinges. Stare into the dim past.
Taste dust dancing in light beams that leak
where shingles gap like teeth that didn't last.

Smell leather seasoned with horse sweat,
blankets lined with variegated hair crust.
Straighten a reluctant latigo strap. Let
your thumbnail scratch cinch ring rust.

Hear tarnished bit chains on a stiff headstall
rattle, lifted from a used-horseshoe hook
nailed to the warped, weathered wood wall.
Read the brittle pages of an old book.

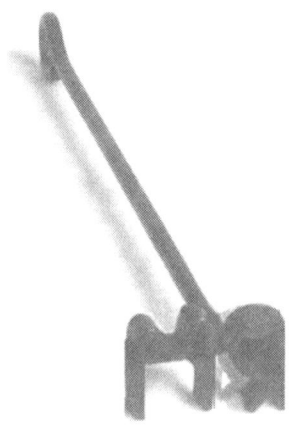

Things a COWBOY SEES *and other poems*

The Rodeo Road

Bad Road

Rod Miller

It isn't the miles, at least not only.
And it isn't just the roads that are lonely.
It's yet another wrinkled shirt.
The stink of the cream that soothes the hurt.
Grease on your pants from the gate on the chute
and another hole in the sole of your boot.

It isn't the miles, at least not only.
And it isn't just the roads that are lonely.
It's a horse, stiff-legged from moving on wheels.
Sick anticipation of paper-wrapped meals.
86 feet of broken ropes.
12-second runs, 9-second hopes.

It isn't the miles, at least not only.
And it isn't just the roads that are lonely.
It's two quarts low, a threadbare tire,
a missing gas cap, a door latched with wire.
The ire of foreign-born motel clerks
over a credit card that no longer works.

It isn't the miles, at least not only.
And it isn't just the roads that are lonely.
It's roll after roll of adhesive tape
hoping your riding arm maintains its shape.
Sore muscles, skinned knuckles, aching bones.
tense conversations on coin-operated phones.

It isn't the miles, at least not only.
And it isn't just the roads that are lonely.
It's radio stations fading away in the night.
18-wheelers roaring by on the right.
Too many hours alone with your thoughts,
replaying your fears until your love rots.

It isn't the miles, at least not only.
And it isn't just the roads that are lonely.
It's willing arms, a drunken embrace.
Bloodshot eyes in an unfamiliar face.
It isn't the miles, at least not only.
And it isn't just the roads that are lonely.

Rod Miller

Rodeo Regina

With vaseline on their teeth
and hair spray in their hatbands
they ride into the light.
Churning hooves stir the crowd
in a quick elliptical trip
around the arena.
Two-finger salutes sprinkle
spectators, flipped from brims
of hats in synthetic colors.
Polished ponies shine
through checkerboard rumps
and braided tails,
haughty atop painted toenails
and fluorescent stockings.
Sequins sparkles spangles
and satin sashes flash in
wide eyes of agog young girls
in the grandstand
who find meaning
in this thing called Queening.

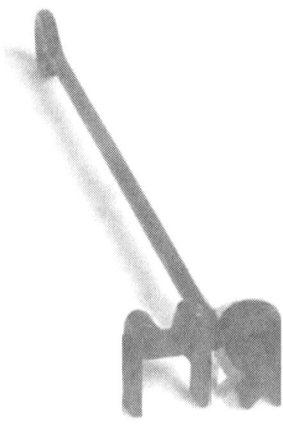

Things a COWBOY SEES *and other poems*

Landing Gear

I can (and do) go on at some length
about my rodeo days
and the sad fact is, both they and I
look better through the passing years' haze.
But the truth of it all can be summed up
in a lot fewer words than that:
my bronc riding career, when all's said and done,
sure was hard on hats.

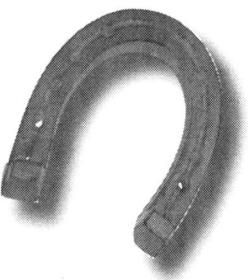

Why I'm Not a Roper
Rod Miller

Give me a twine
and I'll do just fine
at building a loop and spinning;
jumping out of the saddle
and flanking cattle
for wrapping and half-hitching.

The problem I've seen
comes in between
and it's bothered me forever.
I can rope, of course,
or ride the horse—
but I can't do both together.

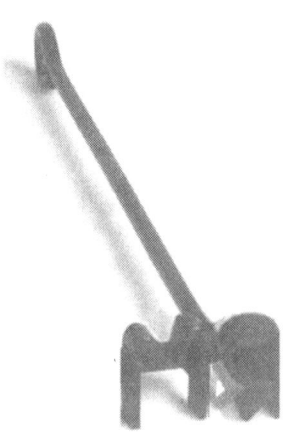

Rodeo Rhythm

There are no eight second
melodies composed
or a conductor's wand
tracing lilting tunes.

No melodious brass,
sweet lyrical strings,
or trilling woodwinds pass
this way—through chute gates.

But that is not to say
there is no music
when broncs and cowboys play.
Percussion! Heels pound

hide. Chaps snap. Spurs chatter.
Shanks pummel shoulders.
Bones rattle. Teeth clatter
as hoofbeats drum dirt.

Slam banging hammer whack.
Jerking jolt. Wrenching
roll. Pulsing thumping crack
when Mach thunders by.

A beat you can dance to.
Toe-tap harmony.
Tapped off. Nothing to do
but do the two-step

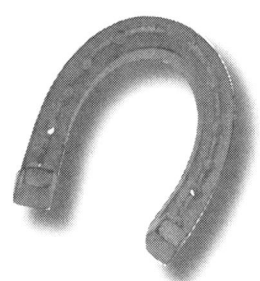

to a Tito Puente
tempo. Stroke and poke
music you play and lay
and hang and rattle.

Things a COWBOY SEES *and other poems*
Looper Blues

Quick roping.
Fast loping
calf all strain and fight.

Wet arenas.
Cheap cantinas.
No bed for the night.

High mile count
hard on mount;
tread on tires slight.

Long score lines
big bovines
judges with bad sight.

Worn-out ropes.
Damaged hopes.
Confidence a fright.

Fifth once more,
they pay four;
wallet getting light.

So it goes
at rodeos—
my complaints are trite.

Rod Miller

Womb to Tomb
For Marlowe

Two hearts. One beats steady
and strong. The other races by.
Confinement presses knee
against rib, back to thigh.

Sounds, muffled and distant,
penetrate. Irresistible, the urge.
Pull. Squeeze. Slide. Every muscle
tense, you nod and emerge;

delivered into chaotic glare
assaulted by motion and sound.
Bull bellows. Brain blows.
Body, unbound, seeks ground.

Face down in arena dirt
consciousness goes astray
as flooding blood erodes neurons
and synapses wash away.

Tucked, now, into the coffin of
a body cold and unresponsive;
rolling through years gathering
dust as memories weave

tapestries of rounders and rodeo,
broncs and bulls—of life before
a hemorraghic stroke of bad luck
drew you out to ride no more.

Things a COWBOY SEES *and other poems*
Long May it Wave

The Star Spangled Banner inspires all manner
of feelings in folks when it plays—
every bareback bronc veteran feels a rush of
    adrenaline
long after his rodeo days.

The Anthem's first sound brings the Chute Boss
    around
yellin' "Pull 'em down boys! Let's rodeo!"
And you straddle the chute, ease down onto the
    brute,
grab your riggin' and stretch latigo.

Then the rockets' red glare, the bombs bursting in
    air
grow distant; seem to fade into dim.
Rosin squeaks in your handhold. The horse shivers
    as if cold.
And, for eight seconds, there's just you and him.

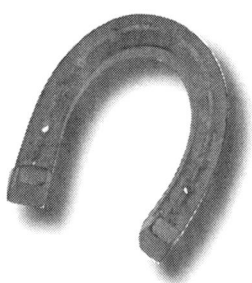

Rod Miller

Luck
(But Not Exactly the Beginner's Kind)

Jammed together in the truck seat
a cowboy, his wife, and three kids
wearing raggedy pants and patched-up boots
and passed-down, worn-out lids.

The pickup truck shuddered to a stop.
It had a stock rack in the back.
And, there among the feed bags and salt,
was a sorry collection of tack.

He rooted through the refuse
of days spent tending cattle
and pulled out from under a pile of twine
an ancient association saddle.

An old canvas bag came out next,
it, too, had seen better days;
so had the bareback rigging inside
and the bull rope, old, and frayed.

He dumped his gear behind the chutes
and hustled to the other end
to arrange to borrow a bulldogging horse
from a long-time, long-lost friend.

The other contestants snickered
at this hand who rode in from the range.
They'd never seen such equipment:
old, outdated, and strange.

Then he kicked the hair off his bareback
and ended up in second place,
beat 'em in the bronc and bull riding,
came in fourth in the steer wrestling race.

They didn't know that years ago
he'd been a star on the college circuit,
but married and went back home to the ranch
to help his family work it.

Just now, there was a note coming due
and hospital bills left by his dad,
so this cowboy showed up at the rodeo
because he needed a payday real bad.

He gathered his family and collected his checks
and limped off in that rusty old truck,
while the cocky young cowboys he'd bettered that
    day
laughed it off as nothing but luck.

Rod Miller

Ranked Among the Top 15 Automobiles of All Time

The trunk smells of rosin and dirty shirts
mixed with horse sweat and arena dirt
and gear bags and boots and used blue jeans
and dirty socks stirred in with the clean.
To open the lid you need a pair of pliers;
the lock is sprung and fastens with wire.

The mirrors are broken off both sides.
The passenger door don't open too wide.
The back seat's full of bottles and cans
and a stolen pillow from a motel in Cheyenne.
Cheeseburger wrappers carpet the floors,
day sheets and ticket stubs round out the décor.

The paint's chipped. It's covered with dents.
Front bumper's missing; the back one's bent.
The odometer quit at two hundred thousand miles.
And it's long since out if it was ever in style.
Every time he gets in, my traveling pal squawks
and I ask every time if he'd rather walk.

Not too many cowboys ask us for rides
and no respectable woman will get inside.
But I'll keep this old junker as long as it runs
because in my eyes this heap is second to none
—I've gone down the road in lots of other cars
and this is the only one that got me to the NFR.

Things a COWBOY SEES *and other poems*

Number 16

It happened in nineteen and seventy-three,
the twenty-third day of June.
It was a Saturday night, under the lights
and a quarter of the waning moon.

Nary a cloud was in the sky,
the stars burned clear and bright,
sixty-nine degrees, a hint of a breeze;
for rodeo, a near-perfect night.

Pawing the bottom of chute number three
stood a horse, fifteen hands two,
the number 16 read on his hip clean,
burned in hair a rich, roan blue.

A white star winked on his forehead
through a forelock tangled and long;
a mane of black, a stripe down his back,
dark bottoms on legs thick and strong.

He rattled the slide gate with a solid kick
when the flank man hooked the strap
and kept up the fight as the rigging pulled tight,
relieving chute boards of pineknots and sap.

Finally the cowboy nodded his face
and the gate cracked open, then wide.
Off flew his hat as 16 whipped out flat
and took a run with a choppy stride.

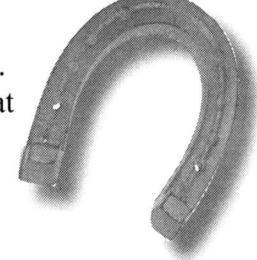

He planted his forefeet and sucked it back
after covering fifty-three feet.
The cowboy's nose advanced past his toes,
but he managed to keep his seat.

Then that big blue roan jumped straight up,
must have been nine feet in the air,
he bellered and roared, lifted off twice more;
liked to bucked off all his white hair.

Next he spun to the left four turns and a half,
got that cowboy away from his hand,
down in the well where he hung for a spell
while looking for a place to land.

16 trotted off with his head in the air,
nostrils flared and tail flying straight;
followed the course of a bay pickup horse
out back through the catch pen gate.

It was as fine a display of the bucking art
as this fan ever has seen;
I've watched hundreds pitch, the best of which
was that blue roan, number 16.

The cowboy's name? I can't recall.
Wish I could, but memory fails.
That rodeo, you know, was a long time ago.
You can't expect me to remember details.

IV
Roundups and Trail Drives

Rod Miller

Rhyme of the Ancient Trail Drive

Cattle, cattle, everywhere
raising dust with thousands of feet;
beef on the hoof for miles around,
more than a city could eat.

Rump roasts as far as the eye can see
from my vantage point in the saddle,
steaks and chops and racks of ribs
on the trail as a herd of cattle.

Filets and sirloins and briskets are
everywhere, there for the takin'—
yet meal after meal, day after day,
they feed us beans and bacon.

Things a COWBOY SEES *and other poems*
Brother's Keeper

    Thunderbolts rip the skies!
Grab yer holts! Night horse flies.
    Cattle dash, horns afire.
Raindrops splash. Muck and mire.
    Cloven feet cut and tear.
Death's drumbeat raises hair.
    Varmint holes. Pony falls!
Cowboy rolls. Devil calls.
    Turn and mill. Gather strays.
Grave on hill. Trail boss prays.
    Push 'em on! Dry yer tears.
Brother's gone. Killer steers!
    Turned sixteen last July.
Things unseen caught his eye.
    Mama cried; begged him No!
Papa's pride told him, Go!
    Followed me up the trail;
I's to see that he not fail.
    I fell short. Watched him die.
I'll report. Watch Ma cry.

Rod Miller
COWBOY COFFEE

You can converse over cappuccino
or sip espresso and latté
but when it comes to drinking coffee,
that just ain't the cowboy way.

Cowboys like it so black and strong
just drinking it tests your might.
And thick enough that your spoon will float
or after stirring, stand upright.

Brewing it ain't no big thing,
you don't need a percolator
or one of them fancy drip machines
or a grinder, mill, or grater.

Just boil some river water
and a big handful of grounds,
both of which you add to
as the level in the pot goes down.

If you want some extra body
throw in some used horseshoes,
and now and then to rich it up
add a pinch of snoose.

That's how real cowboys like their coffee,
and they can't seem to get enough.
Maybe that's why I ain't much of a hand—
I never touch the stuff.

Things a COWBOY SEES *and other poems*

OUTLAW

The dust cloud
chased the horsemen
across the valley floor,
gave up the pursuit
and settled down
to lie in wait some more.

Shaded up
beneath a cedar tree
he watched them, nonchalant.
This sort of thing
he'd seen before—he knew
just what they'd want.

For more years
than he cared to remember
they had tried to bring him in.
They'd string him up,
he knew for sure,
as payment for his sin.

While the others
spent the winters in town
lying about and eating hay,
he stayed out there in the desert—
following the herd
just wasn't his way.

He'd fought them off
when cornered,
backed them down in fear;
with fifteen hundred pounds
behind his horns
he looked more bull than steer.

But more often than not
he'd show them his tail
and beat them in every race,
trotting off into the sand dunes
whenever horseback
cowboys gave chase.

While the horses would sink
in the windblown sand
the overgrown hooves of the steer
held him up like snowshoes,
and, as they'd flounder,
he'd run like a deer.

Maybe it was his size
or his cunning,
perhaps his hideous feet,
or it could have been
just plain good luck
that kept him from being meat.

But as the cowboys rode off
through Tintic Valley,
a dust cloud bringing up the rear,
the old outlaw watched
from the shade of a tree—
free for another year.

Rod Miller

Tabula Rasa

> *Written their history stands*
> *on tablets of stone in the churchyards.*
> —from "Evangeline"
> by Henry Wadsworth Longfellow

Lost somewhere on the empty plains
is a low spot that puddles when it rains,
hinting at the location of my bones.
The only mark, the only impression,
I left on earth is this small depression
out where the prairie wind moans.
    Out where the prairie wind moans.

Into my grave corruption followed,
leaving a corpse empty and hollowed;
a cage of vacant bones wormed clean.
Dirt trickled down to fill the space,
Terra Firma subsided o'er my resting place
out where the prairie winds keen.
    Out where the prairie winds keen.

All the way west in a broken line
forgotten, sunken graves like mine
are the only witness of our demise.
No rubbings, then, to reveal the tale
of we who died on the pioneer trail
out where the prairie wind cries.
    Out where the prairie wind cries.

Of granite tablets there are no traces;
no marble crosses mark the places
of our rest by the westering trail.
No dates carved for death and birth,
only a shallow in the silent earth
out where the prairie winds wail.
    Out where the prairie winds wail.

Trail Driving Days

Rod Miller

Sleep-smeared faces,
propped on squatted bones stiff
from a short night of ground sleeping,
reflect campfirelight.

Tin cups of sludge warm
hovering noses and slow fingers
as bolted breakfast beans and biscuits
weigh heavy.

They gather still-damp saddle blankets,
heft kacks—starlight shimmering
on seats buffed by miles of pants polish—
and drag spurs frosted with dew
to the remuda.

Ornery broncs crowhop,
land stifflegged and heavy,
send shockwaves of amplified gravity
through rattled teeth and pained brains
contemplating another day.

Another day.

Another ten miles, twelve miles,
ambling across virgin grass
soon to be pounded down to dust
and fouled with the effluent
of two-and-a-half thousand head

and a handful of cowboys
wishing, for thirteen days now,
for a bath and a bed and
a morning already washed in sunshine.

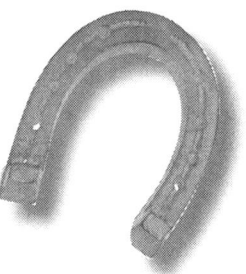

Rod Miller
The Cowboy Trail

From below the Mexican border
to the medicine line and beyond,
cattle country spreads far and wide
and the cowboy trail is long.

*And the cowboy trail is long.
The cowboy trail is long.*

The trail's awash, a river of mud.
A splash the hoofbeat's sound.
The blue of the sky bleaches away
as clouds cascade to the ground.

*And the cowboy trail is long.
The cowboy trail is long.*

Fetlock-deep dust sifted fine as flour
paints every horse on the trail the same.
Sweat disappears, its work undone,
the sky hot and bright as a flame.

*And the cowboy trail is long.
The cowboy trail is long.*

Icy lace trims mountain streams.
You drop the cinch and strip your kack
at the end of a day riding leafy trails.
Steam rises from your horse's back.

> *And the cowboy trail is long.*
> *The cowboy trail is long.*

The trail fades, the horizon is lost
out there where white meets white.
Snow squeaks underfoot as you ride,
chilled bones creak when you alight.

> *And the cowboy trail is long.*
> *The cowboy trail is long.*

From prairie swells to ocean waves,
alpine forests to brushy plains;
wherever the trail leads to cattle,
a cowboy will take up the reins.

> *And a cowboy will take up the reins.*
> *A cowboy will take up the reins.*

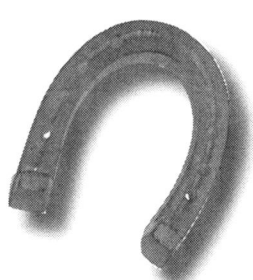

V
Making a Hand

Rod Miller

Cowboy, Defined

What qualities make a man a Cowboy?
Which factor leads the way?
Is it a hell-for-leather attitude,

whether on the job or at play?
Maybe it's having cow sense,
or knowing the mind of a horse.

Or intuitively seeing the lay of the land
and charting the natural course.
The ability to smell a storm on the wind

when there's nary a cloud in the sky;
riding back through the herd knowing
something's amiss, if not knowing what or why.

Or living outdoors in all kinds of weather
eating bad food but staying fit, and strong.
Getting up early and staying up late,

sharing campfire stories and song.
Perhaps it's treating the ladies as such
and always trying to do what's right,

being willing to stand up for what he believes
even when it comes down to a fight.
It could be any or all of these things

by which the true Cowboy is defined.
But to my way of thinking, the thing
that counts most is having a cast iron behind.

Things a COWBOY SEES *and other poems*

PACKSADDLE
For Mother, on her 80th Birthday

No cinches, latigos, or breeching.
No sawbuck tree. No pannier or kyack.
No diamond hitch in a lash rope.
No load stacked or packed on her back.

But when she'd sit, if she'd sit,
between this chore, this job or that,
the bend in the middle made
a lap where, always, something sat:

a bag of groceries back from town,
a book to read, an afghan to crochet,
dresses to hem, shirts to mend,
potatoes to peel, homework to okay.

And babies, owned or borrowed.
Her children, then children grand and great;
family, friends, neighbors, strangers
snuggle up soft and safe and warm and wait

while the packsaddle lap rides them
gently, rocks them easily, down the trail
to dreamland. But no nap for the lap;

it moves on, like a mochilla packing the mail.

Rod Miller

Resolution

Late sun peeks through round-corral rails
where, out of sight of other eyes, I ride
the Roman-nose roan colt that never fails
to dust me. Stupid and stubborn I hide,

alone, pulling futile leather, reins wove
among fingers, rowels stitched into cinch.
Dancing like spit on a sheet-iron stove
he pumps sunlight beneath me by the inch

till the saddle sees more air than me there.
Out-waiting the pain, I lie in the dirt.
And lie to myself. Say I don't care
if I don't ride this horse. That it don't hurt,

that echoing laughter. But in low light
I pause on hands and knees. Find my feet.
Stagger in pride and privacy to the fight,
surrendering sense to stirrup and seat.

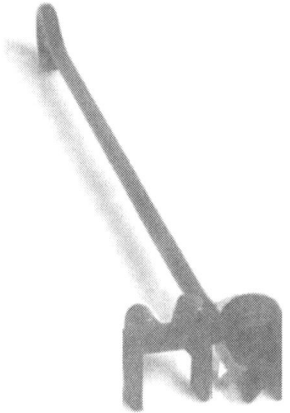

Things a COWBOY SEES *and other poems*

The Staff of Life

Prancing and yapping like impatient pups,
boys watch a loaf still wisping stove smoke
tumble onto the table, then tear into it like
savage starving slavering wolves, for slowpoke

appetites go unsatisfied. Steaming fistfuls
of freshest bread, slathered soggy with hand-
cranked butter and home-bottled berry jam;
all packing the same ranch woman's brand.

She always made a hand, whether with
kitchen kettle or castrating knife, horseback
on the mountain or afoot in the shearing pen,
camp cooking in summer or feeding a stack

of winter hay. One day the horn of a saddle
cinch-strapped to a suddenly upside-down
green-broke colt punched the light out of
LaRee like the ball of her fist punching down

bread dough on baking day. But she, leavened
by grit and laughter and heart and tears and pain
instead of sourdough, could not rise again.
Now, bread comes cold, wrapped in cellophane.

About the Author

Born and raised in a small town in Utah among horses and cattle, and a veteran of the rodeo arena, Rod Miller comes by his love of the West honestly.

A versatile writer, he is author of two nonfiction books, *John Muir: Magnificent Tramp* and *Massacre at Bear River: First, Worst, Forgotten*, and a Western novel, *Gallows for a Gunman*. He has also written many short stories, magazine articles, and book reviews.

His poems have been published in numerous magazines and anthologies. A student of the ingredients of poetry, he also writes essays and conducts workshops on creating poetry.

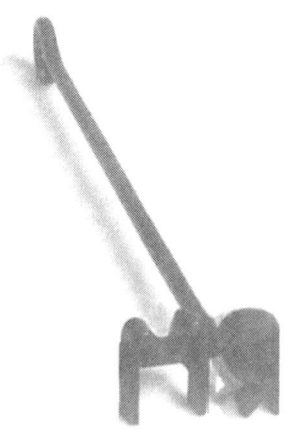

Harris County Public Library
Houston, Texas

CPSIA information can be obtained at www.ICGtesting.com
Printed in the USA
BVOW040622270412

288790BV00001BA/5/P

[8]